W9-CAJ-588

DEMCO

CORN BELT HARVEST

RAYMOND BIAL

Houghton Mifflin Company   Boston   1991.

Central Rappahannock Regional Library
1201 Caroline Street
Fredericksburg, VA 22401

3695806

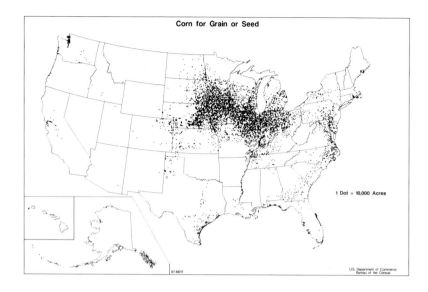

Corn for Grain or Seed

1 Dot = 10,000 Acres

U.S. Department of Commerce
Bureau of the Census

87-M217

*Distribution of corn
in the United States.
Each dot represents
ten thousand acres.*

For Anna and Sarah

I would like to thank the people who appear briefly, yet enduringly, in these photographs, especially the employees of Grand Prairie Co-op Elevator at Ivesdale.

I would also like to express my sincere appreciation to Kyle Wittler and Bob Ulbrich for reviewing the manuscript and to my editor, Mary Lee Donovan, for ably and patiently working with me through several revisions.

Map courtesy of U.S. Department of Commerce, Bureau of the Census

Library of Congress Cataloging-in-Publication Data

Bial, Raymond.
   Corn Belt harvest / Raymond Bial.
     p. cm.
   Summary: Text and photographs describe the United States Corn Belt region and its harvest season.
   ISBN 0-395-56234-1
   1. Corn—Middle West—Juvenile literature. [1. Corn.]
I. Title.   91-392
SB191.M2B49 1991   CIP
633.1'5'0977—dc20   AC

Copyright © 1991 by Raymond Bial

All rights reserved. For information about permission to reproduce selections from this book, write to Permissions, Houghton Mifflin Company, 2 Park Street, Boston, Massachusetts 02108.

Printed in the United States of America

HOR 10 9 8 7 6 5 4 3 2 1

Corn is the most abundant grain in the Western Hemisphere, and it ranks third in the world after rice and wheat.

The United States produces more than half of the corn grown in the world, and more than three-fourths of this corn is grown in the region known as the Corn Belt.

The Corn Belt spreads over western Ohio, Indiana, Illinois, Iowa, Minnesota, Missouri, Nebraska, and South Dakota. Michigan and Wisconsin also produce significant amounts of corn.

In winter, the furrows of black soil are often filled with snow, giving the fields a dappled appearance.

In the Corn Belt the plains stretch beyond sight. Many farmers plow their fields in the autumn, after last year's crops have been harvested. During the winter months the land lies black and dormant. As the days gradually warm toward spring, farmers disk and plant the expansive fields.

A plume of dust is raised behind a disk as the tractor pulls it across the fields.

The wide swath of the disks and planters have allowed farmers to reduce the number of passes they must make.

In the early years of this century, most farms in the Corn Belt were still small, usually 80 to 120 acres. Even a large family could barely keep up with the work. Much of the labor was done with horses or by hand. Now, with huge tractors and implements, a single farmer can manage a thousand or more acres.

The sharp edges of the disks help break up the soil.   *A farmer loads seed corn into the planter.*

Most of the corn in the Midwest is planted in rows. The machine drops the seeds individually at any desired spacing, usually 30 to 36 inches apart.

Prior to and during planting, farmers hope for dry weather so that their tractors won't bog down in muddy fields. Once the corn has been planted, however, they wish for rain.

Late in the afternoon, a tractor stands ready as the planter is loaded with seed.

Corn requires soil with good tilth. Tilth is the ability of the soil to aggregate, or hold together. Good contact between the seed and the soil is essential for proper germination of the seed corn. If the soil is too loose, like sand, it will not adequately retain moisture. At the same time, the soil must be friable. That is, it must readily crumble in the hand.

Corn is planted in long, perfectly straight rows to make cultivation and harvest as simple and efficient as possible. Farmers use a cultivator, a chisel-toothed implement that is pulled behind a tractor, to scrape under the weeds along the rows.

By late spring, tender young leaves of corn begin to emerge from the black soil, forming delicate green lines through the fields. As the days get warmer, the corn grows more quickly, and by early June, the plains are completely overtaken by green.

The unusual-looking highboy can spray a band forty to sixty feet wide on each pass.

At midsummer, when the corn is too tall to be cultivated, it may be sprayed to control weeds or insects with a machine called a highboy. Riding above the corn, the highboy speeds over the fields spraying a wide swath of rows at a time.

Farmers may also apply herbicides and insecticides at planting time. However, some farmers are becoming aware of the damage these chemicals cause to wildlife, people, and the environment. They are trying to cut down on their use and are supporting research to develop ecologically sound products.

Summer in the Midwest can be measured by the height of the corn. Farmers used to say that the corn should be "knee-high by the Fourth of July." But these days, the corn is head-high by then. With an average rainfall of 8 to 10 inches during the five months of the growing season — roughly from mid-May through mid-October — and daily temperatures in July between 70 and 80 degrees Fahrenheit, the Corn Belt provides excellent growing conditions.

Tassels stand out against the blue of the summer sky. At right, silk spills from an ear of corn.

Winter suddenly seems long past. Its quiet has been replaced by the rustle of corn leaves across thousands and thousands of acres.

Leaves appear all along the length of the plant, which may have one or two ears of corn. Brace roots extend in a circle around the plant and help support the stalk. The corn plant is topped with a tassel from which pollen grains fall onto the silk emerging from the potential ears. These threads of corn silk aid in pollination.

Ears of dent corn lying in the field at harvest time. Note the slight indentation in each kernel.

We are all familiar with juicy sweet corn, which gains its name and its taste from its high sugar content. We are also well acquainted with popcorn. However, dent corn, commonly called field corn, is the most widely planted of the six kinds of corn. In fact, 90 percent of all corn grown in the United States is dent corn. And nearly two-thirds of all the corn grown in the United States, including most of the dent corn, is used for livestock feed.

Signs at the roadside invite farmers to stop and inspect varieties of hybrid corn in a test plot.

By the time Europeans were introduced to corn, Native Americans had already experimented with its development. Corn has been improved so much that it no longer exists in the wild. At least 95 percent of the corn grown in the United States consists of hybrids. These varieties have been inbred over several generations and then crossbred to ensure strong, disease-resistant, and high-yielding crops. The development of hybrid corn and mechanized farming methods have led to an increase in yields in the United States, from 25 bushels per acre in the 1930s to an average of 120 bushels an acre in 1990.

Total corn production in the United States has increased from 2.3 billion bushels annually in the 1930s to over 8 billion bushels a year. Fully one-quarter of all the cropland in the United States is devoted to corn.

The colors of an autumn sunrise match the golds and yellows of the sprawling fields of corn.

Summer always slips quickly past in the Corn Belt, and by August the corn stands at least seven feet tall. As you drive down the back roads, walls of corn rise up on either side of you. The horizon is now just a memory; you have to stop at every crossroad and look carefully in each direction, because oncoming drivers can't see you, and you can't see them.

Late in the afternoon, the light of the setting sun gleams on the stalks.

The approach of first frost sends the corn into a sudden transformation, the uniformly green stalks and leaves fading to light brown. The ears of corn tip under their own weight and dangle from the stalks. The dry leaves now rustle, like the sound of the ocean in a shell. Against the sprawl of tan fields, the sky has never appeared so blue.

Ears of ripe corn hang from the stalks, ready to be harvested.

In late autumn farmers wait for the corn to dry down sufficiently for harvest. The wetter the corn, the longer it must be dried down in storage bins on the farm or at the elevator. This means farmers pay more for natural gas or electricity needed to power the dryers.

Farmers are always at the mercy of the weather. As in the planting, if it rains during the harvest, the fields may become so soft that the heavy machinery gets stuck. High winds may knock down stalks, resulting in significant crop loss. There is also the possibility of ice storms and even heavy snow.

Although most farmers use the latest technology available, some still prefer corn pickers.

Once the conditions are right for harvest, a sudden explosion of activity follows, as virtually every field is set upon by combines. Trucks and wagons emerge from sheds and barns to carry the harvest from field to elevator.

Corn was once picked by hand and later by machines simply called corn pickers, like the one above. Most farmers now use combines, which not only pick and shuck but also shell the ears of corn right in the field.

With dry weather, the combines make easy work of the cornfields.

At harvest time, trucks and wagons line the roads across the Corn Belt.

Like a hungry monster, the combine steadily eats its way through the corn.

During the autumn harvest, ripe corn fills the plains. As you travel up and down the roads, you can see ears nodding on the stalks or being snatched by the teeth of the combines. You can see the shelled corn pouring out of the combines in a steady stream of bright yellow or heaped up on the backs of trucks lumbering down the country roads.

This combine harvests eight rows of corn at a time. Others may harvest as few as four or as many as twelve.

Fitted onto the front of the combine, cornheads guide the stalks into rollers, which gather, shuck, and shell the corn. The combine quickly fills with shelled corn, leaving crushed stalks and leaves scattered on the ground behind it.

The enclosed cab of a combine
offers shade to the driver
and protects him from dust
and extreme heat.

Tinted windows reduce glare,
helping the operator, who must
keep the combine pointed
straight down the rows of corn.

The unloading auger, rotating like a corkscrew, draws corn up along its spiral blades.

Usually, the operator is able to make one "pass," or trip, down the rows and back again before the combine is filled with corn. The combine is then drawn alongside a truck or a wagon, its unloading auger rotated over the wagon, and the load of corn transferred.

A combine operator waits as his load of corn is transferred into a truck.

An auger draws corn from the hopper, a box-shaped storage unit fitted atop the combine.

It takes only a few minutes to transfer corn from the combine to a truck or wagon. Then the operator steers the combine down the rows again.

The combining continues until the trucks and wagons are heaped with shelled corn. Then the corn is transported to a grain elevator, where it will be stored.

With the combine picking as many as eight rows of corn at a pass, it doesn't take long to fill a wagon.

Standing at the edge of the field, these wagons will soon be on their way to the elevator.

Here a farmer has chosen to store his corn on the farm.

An auger powered by his tractor carries a stream of corn into a storage bin.

Ears of harvested corn used to be stored in cribs, which were naturally ventilated.

Most corncribs are now abandoned or are used to store machinery.

The concrete bins at the elevator stand ready to receive the harvest of corn.

Always located beside railroad tracks, modern grain elevators rise up in many small towns throughout the Midwest. With their strong, vertical lines, they appear out of place on the plains, where most everything, notably the distant horizon, tends toward the horizontal. You can ride in a small cage to the top of the elevators, where you can see for miles across the flat land.

A worker in the elevator office waits for the first loads of corn to arrive.

Elevators are groups of cylinders made of poured concrete. When they are constructed, the work continues nonstop until all the concrete is poured to avoid any seams or cracks in each cylinder.

Most elevators are part of large companies which may own four or five to as many as thirty or forty elevators in a particular region.

The arm of a vacuum is poised over a truck, ready to take a sample.

As the harvest accelerates, trucks begin to line up at the elevator office. Each of the loaded vehicles is weighed at the scale in front of the office. The weight of the empty wagon or truck is subtracted from the total weight to determine the weight of the load of corn.

While the trucks are on the scales, an arm is dipped into the corn and a small sample vacuumed through a pipe and into a small box inside the elevator office.

The clerk in the elevator office pours kernels of corn onto the scale.

The sample of incoming corn is dropped into a pan. It is then weighed and its moisture content determined. If the moisture content is 20 percent or higher, the farmer will be charged a drying fee to bring it down to 15.5 percent.

After the corn is weighed and a moisture sample is taken, the trucks move down the road to the elevator storage area.

As the truck bed is tilted backward, the corn spills into a pit. In just a minute or two, the truck is empty and heading back to the fields for more corn.

Lit up by the morning sun, corn splatters on the grate of the pit.

At the elevator storage areas, the corn is dumped into a pit covered with a grate. It is then drawn into the tall elevators by augers through a complex system of pipes.

Throughout the day, one load of corn after another is dumped into the pits. Trucks and wagons often must line up to wait their turn. There is barely enough time for workers to sweep up around the pit before the next truck pulls up.

Elevator workers are kept busy throwing open tailgates, scraping out truckbeds, and sweeping up around the pits.

An elevator worker squints to keep the dust out of his eyes.

Another load of corn is dumped into the pit, creating an explosion of dust and chaff.

The elevator continues to accept corn until well after dusk.

The corn collects briefly on the grate over the pit.

Everywhere corn gleams brightly in the sunlight. As long as the weather holds, the harvest continues for twelve hours or more each day. Even working these long hours, it may take two to four weeks to bring it all in.

Elevator workers look on as another load of corn pours into the pit.

If it rains, the harvest may be delayed for several days because the fields are too wet for the combines. Otherwise the harvest continues nonstop Monday through Sunday, until all of the corn is harvested.

Trucks appear very small next to the tall storage bins of an elevator.

It doesn't take long for each storage bin to get filled with corn.

Because it is so fine, grain dust is as volatile as flammable gas.

While the corn is stored at the elevator, moisture samples are frequently taken, because the corn must be kept dry. It must also be kept clean and maintained at the right temperature.

Farmers and elevator operators take great pride in their products and carefully monitor the corn not only to protect their investment, but also to deliver the highest quality corn to their customers.

This panel of controls is used to operate the complicated system of fans and dryers.

These gauges help to monitor the moisture of the corn and the power supply.

Train cars line the tracks at an elevator.

The corn that is not fed to livestock may be processed in mills throughout the Midwest to serve a wide variety of uses. The corn and its by-products are transported by train all over the United States or shipped by barge down the Mississippi River to New Orleans. From there, they are exported around the world. Corn and other agricultural produce are major exports.

We are all familiar with corn on the cob, popcorn, canned corn, and other foods that feature corn, such as breakfast cereals. Some other products in which corn is used are ketchup, ice cream, candies, sausage, and margarine.

Corn syrup, or dextrose, is widely used as a sweetener. Corn oil is used in cooking and salad oils. Cornstarch is used to thicken a variety of foods, such as puddings and gravies. Starches are used in chewing gum and candies such as jelly beans. They are also often used in the textile industry for sizing, or stiffening, clothes. Papers, cosmetics, batteries, explosives, synthetic rubber, plastics, and many other, sometimes unlikely, products also have corn as one of their constituents.

Pink from sunburns, these hogs gobble up large quantities of corn each day.

If prices are low, many farmers raise hogs and feed their corn to them. The hogs will bring a higher market price, resulting in greater profits. This is commonly referred to as marketing your corn through hogs.

If corn prices hold, farmers are able to protect their large investment in land and equipment, as well as to realize a small profit.

Crushed leaves and stalks left in the wake of the combines will be plowed under to restore nutrients to the soil.

With luck and good weather, the harvest comes to an end just as quickly as it began. The fields are picked clean and lie bare in the autumn light.

The combines and trucks are parked in sheds and barns. Farmers are able to relax briefly from their labors. Once again the entire region falls silent. Once again you can see the horizon.

In every season and at every stage of farming, a cornfield, like this one, which has been plowed, can be an interesting and beautiful place.

In anticipation of next year's crop, many farmers plow their fields again. Large tractors churn back and forth. Behind the plow blades, the soil flows in long, black waves.

Soon after, the deep furrows are struck with frost. The ground will not fully thaw again until the following spring.

Deep colors emerge in the sky as the sun sets over the land.

Winter is coming on hard. The land has already taken on a dark cast, which mirrors the shortening days.

As they settle in for the winter, farmers look back at the harvest and a job well done. They also look forward to another growing season with hope and anticipation. To farm on the Corn Belt is to appreciate firsthand the change in seasons, the circle of life.

For Further Reading

Excellent articles about corn are presented in the *Academic American Encyclopedia, World Book Encyclopedia,* and *Encyclopedia Americana,* all of which were sources for this book.

For the most comprehensive book about this subject, readers may wish to consult the third edition of *Modern Corn Production,* by Samuel R. Aldrich, Walter O. Scott, and Robert G. Hoeft, published in 1986 by A & L Publications, Champaign, Ill.

The following books for young people were also used in the preparation of *Corn Belt Harvest,* and readers may enjoy them:

Birch, Beverley. *Let's Look Up Food from Many Lands.* Morristown, N.J.: Silver Burdett, 1986.

Brandenberg, Aliki. *Corn Is Maize: The Gift of the Indians.* New York: Thomas Y. Crowell, 1976.

Elting, Mary, and Folsom, Michael. *The Mysterious Grain.* New York: M. Evans, 1967.

Hammond, Winifred G. *Corn: From Farm to Market.* New York: Coward, McCann & Geoghegan, 1972.

Limburg, Peter R. *The Story of Corn.* New York: Julian Messner, 1971.

Selsam, Millicent E. *The Plants We Eat.* New York: William Morrow, 1981.

Watts, Franklin. *Corn.* Chicago: Children's Press, 1977.